anythink

D0567923

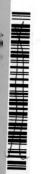

MY CALENDAR:

HOLIDAYS

Luana K. Mitten

Rourke
Publishing LLC
Vero Beach, Florida 32964

www.rourkepublishing.com

PHOTO CREDITS: © snowkoala: Title Page; © Patricia Nelson: page 3; © Kolan: page 3 top; © Jani Bryson: page 3 bottom, 14, 23; © Hans Slegers: page 5 top; © Tim Robbins: page 5, 7, 9 10, 11, 13, 15, 16, 17, 19; © Pamspix: page 6; © Library of Congress: page 8, 16; © Steven Wynn: page 10 left; © Nic Taylor: page 11; © Nicole S. Young: page 12; © Juan Monino: page 13 right, 15 left; © Dar Yang Yan: page 14 background; © DIGIcal: page 15 right; © Catherine Lane: page 17; © U.S. Army: page 18; © Beata Becla: page 19 bottom; © Jamie Carrol: page 19 top; © Lisa Thornberg: page 20; © Leo Kowal: page 21 top; © Marc Dietrich: page 21 middle; © Nic Taylor: page 21 bottom; © Eileen Hart: 22 bottom; © Julie Felton: 22 bottom; © Ali Mazraie Shadi: page 23

Editor: Kelli L. Hicks

Cover design by Nicola Stratford, bdpublishing.com

Interior Design by Heather Botto

Library of Congress Cataloging-in-Publication Data

Mitten, Luana K.
 My calendar : holidays / Luana K. Mitten.
  _p. cm. -- (Concepts)
 ISBN 978-1-60472-412-7
 1. Holidays--United States--Juvenile literature. I. Title.
 GT4803.M58 2009
 394.26973--dc22

                    2008024838

Printed in the USA

CG/CG

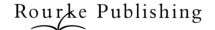

Rourke Publishing

www.rourkepublishing.com – rourke@rourkepublishing.com
Post Office Box 3328, Vero Beach, FL 32964

Each country has its own celebration days, or national holidays. Many schools and businesses close on these days.

In the United States
of America, there are
11 national holidays.

4

On January 1, we celebrate new beginnings. What holiday is it?

JANUARY						
SUNDAY	MONDAY	TUESDAY	WEDNESDAY	THURSDAY	FRIDAY	SATURDAY
1	2	3	4	5	6	7
8	9	10	11	12	13	14
15	16	17	18	19	20	21
22	23	24	25	26	27	28
29	30	31				

5

IT'S NEW YEAR'S DAY!

6

On the third Monday in January, we honor a man who was a civil rights leader. What holiday is it?

"I Have A Dream...that little black boys and black girls will be able to join hands with little white boys and white girls as sisters and brothers.

7

I have a

IT'S MARTIN LUTHER KING, JR. DAY

Martin Luther King, Jr. was born on January 15, 1939.

On January 20, we celebrate Inauguration Day. It's the day we celebrate the election of a new president.

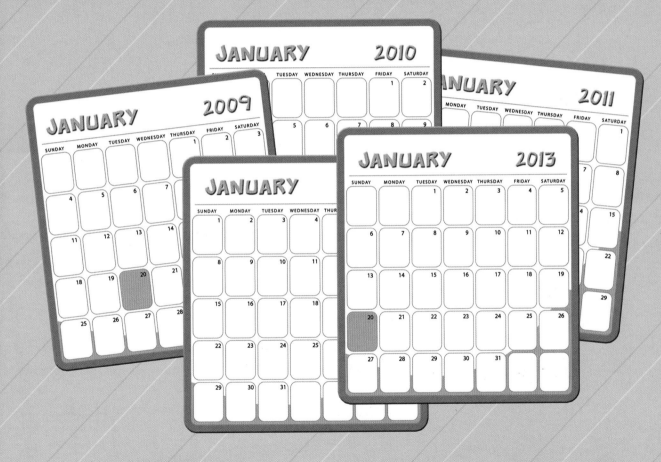

Inauguration Day is the only holiday that is not celebrated every year!

On the third Monday in February, we celebrate President's Day. President's day started as a way to honor our first president, George Washington.

10

FEBRUARY

SUNDAY	MONDAY	TUESDAY	WEDNESDAY	THURSDAY	FRIDAY	SATURDAY
1	2	3	4	5	6	7
8	9	10	11	12	13	14
15	16	17	18	19	20	21
22	23	24	25	26	27	28

George Washington was born on February 22, 1732.

On the last Monday in May, we remember all of the soldiers who died protecting our country.

What holiday is it?

IT'S MEMORIAL DAY.

On July 4, we celebrate the United State's birthday. What holiday is it?

JULY

SUNDAY	MONDAY	TUESDAY	WEDNESDAY	THURSDAY	FRIDAY	SATURDAY
1	2	3	4	5	6	7
8	9	10	11	12	13	14
15	16	17	18	19	20	21
22	23	24	25	26	27	28
29	30	31				

IT'S INDEPENDENCE DAY!

On the first Monday in September, we celebrate Labor Day. It reminds us of how hard people work each day.

SEPTEMBER

SUNDAY	MONDAY	TUESDAY	WEDNESDAY	THURSDAY	FRIDAY	SATURDAY
1	2	3	4	5	6	7
8	9	10	11	12	13	14
15	16	17	18	19	20	21
22	23	24	25	26	27	28
29	30	31				

15

On the second Monday in October, we celebrate Columbus Day in honor of the explorer Christopher Columbus.

16

On November 11, we thank all the people in the military for serving our country.

What holiday is it?

NOVEMBER

SUNDAY	MONDAY	TUESDAY	WEDNESDAY	THURSDAY	FRIDAY	SATURDAY
1	2	3	4	5	6	7
8	9	10	11	12	13	14
15	16	17	18	19	20	21
22	23	24	25	26	27	28
29	30	31				

17

IT'S VETERANS DAY.

On the fourth Thursday in November, we celebrate a special harvest.

What holiday is it?

NOVEMBER

SUNDAY	MONDAY	TUESDAY	WEDNESDAY	THURSDAY	FRIDAY	SATURDAY
1	2	3	4	5	6	7
8	9	10	11	12	13	14
15	16	17	18	19	20	21
22	23	24	25	26	27	28
29	30	31				

19

IT'S THANKSGIVING DAY!

20

The last holiday each year is celebrated by many but not all.

What holiday is it?

DECEMBER

SUNDAY	MONDAY	TUESDAY	WEDNESDAY	THURSDAY	FRIDAY	SATURDAY
1	2	3	4	5	6	7
8	9	10	11	12	13	14
15	16	17	18	19	20	21
22	23	24	25	26	27	28
29	30	31				

IT'S CHRISTMAS DAY!

22

Next time you have a holiday from school, remember why we celebrate the day.

23

Index

Further Reading

Carle, Eric. *The Very Hungry Caterpillar*. Scholastic, 1994.

Rosenstiehl, Agnes. *Silly Lilly and the Four Seasons*. Raw Junior, LLC, 2008.

Ward, Cindy and de Paola, Tomie. *Cookie's Week*. Putnam, 2004.

Recommended Websites

www.ms.k12.il.us/mecc/learning.htm

www.iage.com/kidlink.html

www.fisher-price.com/us/little-people/section.asp?section=ONLINE

About the Author

Luana Mitten lives in Florida with her family. Luana and her son, Louis, like decorating the house for different holidays.

24